Tumbling

poems by

Don Kimball

Finishing Line Press
Georgetown, Kentucky

Tumbling

ACKNOWLEDGMENTS

I would like to thank the following journals for first publishing these poems:

The Meeting House: "Knuckle-head"
The J Journal: "Radio"
Rattle: "Burial for a Stray"
Verse Wisconsin: "Farmer's Lament"

I would also like to give thanks to Rhina Espaillat and the Powow River Poets
for their continuing friendship, generosity, humor, inspiration and, as always,
for providing keen eyes that watched over many of these poems in various
forms. Thanks and gratitude goes out to Robert Crawford, Bill Gleed and the
Hyla Brook Poets for providing the needed oasis in NH for an appreciation
of meter and rhyme in writing poetry; Gibson's Bookstore in appreciation for
providing a poetry-friendly space to host the monthly poetry reading series
sponsored by the Poetry Society of New Hampshire.

For friendship, advice and encouragement, I thank Vicki and Allan, Bonnie,
Phil, Sarah S, Tim, Pieter and Lizette.
Editor: Christen Kincaid

Cover Art: Bonnie Periale

Author Photo: Priscilla Kimball

Cover Design: Elizabeth Maines

Table of Contents

As always, my deepest gratitude goes to my wife, Priscilla, for her enduring kindness and passion that encourages and sustains.

Making My First Getaway, 1947

Awake for three days
with my cries,
you tied my waist
to a gray rock,
half my size.

I'd seen Dad
grab a rock
and plumb a fence post
or block the car
from rolling backward
down the driveway. I
yanked my rock
through alders and mud,
halfway into town ...

before you got
the call
from Mrs. Potts
who'd spotted cars
swerving and
your little boy
along the asphalt,
leaning against the anchor
of that rock.

To See It Go
for M.K.

Odd to see the big old house
with its portico, still there
on top of the hill
like a grand hotel
or landlocked liner.

Easier, perhaps,
to see it go—our house,
skirted by azaleas,
lilacs, rhododendrons
our grandmother planted,
the pond we skated on,
the apple orchard, fields
and woods I roamed—
if, instead, another family
like ours
filling all 14 rooms
with their foibles
and fuss;
someone, like our father,
seeing the lawns get mowed,
replacing shingles, window panes,
scraping, repainting clapboards,
before the house goes ...

the way the barn went,
both ends leaning inward
like folding hands,
collapsing
one day
in a clatter
of dust,
a cellar hole
rimmed by snow.

Farmer's Lament

She milked the cow,
I rode the plow;

She planted seeds,
I pulled the weeds;

She birthed the lambs,
I sheared the rams;

She cleaned our house,
I hunted grouse.

Then, Christmas Day,
Tending the sow,
She passed away.

I'm selling now.

Russell Lott or Current Occupant:

Not to worry;
wherever you are,
ensnared in some far-off plot
or well-off
in witness protection,
we still consider you
one of us.

For My Son

I kneel before you,
as a mother might,
to button your shirt
or tie a shoe,
my son, alert, subdued,
your first train ride

away from home, I could
not hide my tears from you.
The fleeting bullet of a
train leaves me muddled
in this joyless dream,
on a crowded platform,
still conceiving you;
a son I never knew.

Lost and Found
for P.E.K.

Washing my hands, love,
I found your earring,
and wondered why
it was in *my* sink,
instead of yours,
stuck between
the pop-up stopper
and the collerette.
It held on
for nearly 24 hours,
without either of us
spotting it.

Amazing it wasn't tossed
by a cat's paw
or lost
in water
blasting out
of the faucet's
small Niagara,
shoving it past
the hair-clotted tailpiece
to disappear
somewhere
in the maze
of plumbing.

How attached it must be
to your lovely earlobe,
your silver earring, still
dangling
its dainty
hexagonal shield
embossed by
tiny colored stones,
the clasp
grasping!

Knuckle-head

Hijacking
my work
by whacking

his bill
at the roof
of my neighbor's shiny
Cadillac,

the sapsucker's
ruckus
rattles
a battle with pot
and spoon;

its rat-a-tat-tat
a brassy dit-dit-dot
to tag
his territory or
tattoo
a lover's plot.

Flatulent Cows of Rasdorf

It was sparked
by static electricity
from the swishing cow brush
of a massaging machine.
Inside the dairy barn,
which housed ninety cows,
a methane cloud
had been swelling
all week.

Nearly a mile off
we saw
the eerie flash
of flames,
a fiery cypress,
or was it Odin's torch?

According to the *polizei*,
one cow
was treated for minor burns.

Full of the Moon

What do you do when the sun
has lost his place and the moon's
full of herself? That carnival face
troubling the night, her gauzy
luminous glare behind tree limbs
black as guns. Cache your cakes
of honey, there is no place
to hide
except inside,
away from all the windows;
still, you know she's there!

If a Tree Falls in the Forest …

While honeybees hum in noon heat
trees prefer to sit it out
on a granite rock
and talk,
or stretch out across the grass for a midday snooze,
exposing their girth.

At desks, in a classroom, you will not hear
the rustle of their leaves,
limbs gesturing,
as they go on
about forest fires, frost cracks, Dutch Elm, men
with power saws.

Younger trees in need of pruning
lie next to each other, crooning
like lovers lolling on the green; if you
step outside, you might
catch them in a flurry of limbs
going at it,
one birch
on top another.

                    They'll rise, again,
when birds begin their gleaning
in the cool of the late afternoon,
or if a Monarch Tree
sees you lumbering
over the horizon and,
like a crow,
creaks out a clarion call.

In the Cordillera

Under the muddy
tumble of mountain-torrents,
a clatter of stones.

Clop, clop, clop of hooves
across rocks, sea shells, lava.
Sunlight slips away

from the cratered face
of this earth. Deep in cold dark
old stones rattle on.

Park Ranger

*"… thousands of migrating lady beetles, an endless swarm of them,
undulating …"*   Jordan Fisher Smith, *Nature Noir*

Warm, dry and dusty,
the wind picks up, rumbling in
your ears. An amber

haze billows between
you and the scattered birch trees
beyond the cobbled

beach. Hobbling on
pebbles, you step inside this
burnished cloud: a mass

migration of wings,
these lucky lady beetles
almost endlessly

swarm, undulating
up the canyon on the wind.
One by one, they tick

your stiff, broad brimmed hat;
landing on your shirt, crawling
on your sleeves. You turn,

facing these tiny
migrants, do you feel them flow
over you slowly?

Autumn's afternoon
sun glowing through a million
wings like saffron robes.

Keyhole

The late
afternoon light,
a keyhole in mauve clouds,
highlights the sheets of yesterday's
scant snow.

Neighborhood Watch

Aroused
by a cacophony
of curses,
supposing crows
are on to something—
an owl, a fox, a hawk—
I haul out of bed
and, lurching
toward the crack of dawn,
all its racket,
steal across the lawn
toward a stand of cedars
behind my neighbor's house.

Barely feeling the dew
on my toes, I catch
a murder
of crows,
in the cocklight,
mobbing
what looks
like a red-tailed hawk,
when I spot
the widow's face,
pressed against her bedroom window,
eyeing me.

Sonnenizio on a Line from Kim Addonizio

What happened, happened once. So now it's best
we leave, forget it happened. It's for the best;
it only happened just this once, okay?
Why it happened is of no consequence ...
mere happenstance. Don't think too much of this,
it'll leave you unhappy ... only happened once.
I'll say, "it never happened," the humping part,
and let my hapless wife assume we kissed
just once, a mishap of one too many bourbons.
It happens. Let me excuse myself, and please
keep it quiet, okay? So it happened—
the back end slap, a bit of tickle, best
that you and I forget this happened; now leave,
it just so happens she's nuts, but not naïve.

Ogie

It's Sunday morning, and the lawn's unmowed;
neighbor dogs are barking. Ron is tying
his tie, Irene slips on her summer dress
when their willful, half-grown Westie takes off
tailing a trailer-load of jet skis towed
behind a pickup. Only yesterday,
a neighbor caught him chasing off a bear!
The dog just keeps on going; did Irene—
or maybe Ron—forget to turn it on,
that invisible fence? In Sunday clothes
they rush along the street, those steeple bells
beseeching them to hurry up. It's such
a busy road between the towns. Now Ron,
tieless and gasping, there before Irene;
cars slowing down, swerving, driving on.

Burial for a Stray
For B. B.

Two dogs and a cat who knew you best
came by and sat as I dug a hole.
Azaleas bloom there where you rest.
Two dogs, a cat, who knew you best,
keep vigil here: at whose behest?
Torn ear, one eye: life takes its toll.
Two dogs and a cat who knew you best
Came by and sat. I dug the hole.

Radio

What should I do, my love,
when you—nearly twenty years
younger—fly off into the night
pursuing the guy who smashed the rear
window of our new car—what
but reach for that
baseball bat
gathering dust
behind the cellar door?

Suppose you get to him
while I'm still lagging behind,
gasping, and he goads
you into stabbing him
with that greasy steak knife
you grabbed
from the kitchen table
on your way out of the house;
or worse,

when he's unable to pry that thing
loose with his screwdriver
and he's got no use
for his bleeding hand,
another woman
complicating his life,
he turns to you?

Call It My Style

When my wife yells at me,
or calls me a name in derision,
I smile
to avoid a collision.

When my smartass neighbor,
with his bloviations,
tempts me to reconstruct him, I
decline all invitations.

When my mother blurts out, "Don't worry, dear,
you'll get by on charm,"
I thank her for the compliment.
Maybe she means no harm.

When the man she calls my father,
sneers his dissatisfaction,
Sorry, I say.
That's my reaction.

Perhaps walking away
is in my DNA.

Transient Ischemic Attack

Today, after 60 years,
my brain abandoned my right arm
still holding my wallet
high above the counter
as if to signal
for silence
or a waiter.

I glared at my hand, as if
reduced to a relic,

"Put the wallet on the counter!"

My left arm, servant,
supporting actor, brother
buckled my seatbelt
and drove me
to Emergency.

Contretemps

Her fifty-seventh
slips by;

three days later,
she cries

you never even said
a word.

He tries to dash off
a card

to slip beside her favorite
Pinot

when she comes home
from work,

but his nervous tremor, that Richter scale
of age,

turns all his sentiments
to scribbles;

he types a love letter
in Papyrus font,

lays out old photographs to prop
an evening;

reaching for them, she spills
the wine.

Afterlife

Some afterlife! First, you take your time,
traipsing the corridors of Wilton Place,
then leave us battling for what little you
left behind, while maggots feast on
your body's meat! All else that's left of you,
this rocking chair, a ponderous sideboard,
that stodgy grandfather clock, which stopped
its frantic nagging years ago, while
taking a stand against the shadows; all
that's left for us to do, Mother, is grab
what we can get, while we devour you
in bitterness remembered, bit by bit.

Tumbling

down
those cellar stairs
I knew so well,
fumbling, reaching for
what is
not there;

I tried to keep
an open mind,
not waste this moment
brooding on
what I was
leaving
behind ...

except, on the tile floor,
my body stopped,
my elbow, my knees, my shoulder
just couldn't wait
to show me
how I'd dropped,
that much older.

Preoccupied

Lately, I've been
lapsing.
Intending to stash
a dirty serving dish
in our dish washer, I
pull out the drawer
of silverware instead.

No matter.

Just the other night,
holding an empty platter
amid a lot of chit-chat
and clatter of plates,
I find myself
pulling open yet
another drawer, this one
housing all the trash;
I circumnavigate
the house like
a fool on a blind date.

No matter.

If someone asked,
I'm apt to say,
just another poem
I'm working on today.

Born in California, **Don Kimball** spent his childhood on a tree farm in New England. He has a B.A. in English and Philosophy from the University of Arkansas, where he also completed two years of postgraduate work in the Arkansas Creative Writing Program, and an M.S.W. from Smith College School of Social Work. Don is the author of two previous chapbooks *Journal of a Flatlander* (Finishing Line Press, 2009) and *Skipping Stones* (Pudding House Publications, 2008). A longstanding member of the prestigious Powow River Poets in Newburyport, MA and the current president of the Poetry Society of New Hampshire, Don's poetry has appeared in *Blue Unicorn, Dogwood, The Formalist, The Lyric, Rattle* and various other journals. His poems also appear in several anthologies, including *The Powow River Anthology* (Ocean Publishing, 2006), *Fashioned Pleasures: Twenty-Four Poets Play Bouts-Rimés with a Shakespearean Sonnet* (Parallel Press), and *The Other Side of Sorrow* (Poetry Society of New Hampshire). Don lives with his wife and their two wayward cats in Concord, NH and for 10 years has hosted a monthly poetry reading series at Concord's only independent Bookstore.

www.ingramcontent.com/pod-product-compliance
Lightning Source LLC
LaVergne TN
LVHW091236080426
835509LV00009B/1307